PROJECT Citizen

A WE THE PEOPLE PORTFOLIO-BASED PROGRAM

LEVEL 1

Administered by the Center for Civic Education
in cooperation with the National Conference of State Legislatures

We the People: Project Citizen
is directed by the Center for Civic Education
and funded by the U.S. Department of Education under the
Education for Democracy Act approved by the United States Congress.

FOR ADDITIONAL INFORMATION PLEASE CONTACT

Project Citizen
Center for Civic Education
5145 Douglas Fir Road, Calabasas, CA 91302-1440
818.591.9321 FAX 818.591.9330
www.civiced.org

Project Citizen
National Conference of State Legislatures
7700 East First Place, Denver, CO 80230-7143
303.364.7700 FAX 303.364.7800
www.ncsl.org

03 02 01 06 07 08

ISBN 0-89818-198-4

CONTENTS

A NOTE TO READERS

Dear Students, Teachers, and Parents:

We at the Center for Civic Education welcome your participation in **We the People: Project Citizen**, a program in civic education. We hope you will find it interesting and worthwhile.

In the words of Abraham Lincoln, we have inherited a government that is "of the people, by the people, and for the people." Our right to participate in governing ourselves in order to protect our rights and promote our common welfare carries certain responsibilities. Among these responsibilities are the need to develop the knowledge and skills to participate intelligently and the willingness to promote liberty and justice for all people.

We believe this program will add to students' knowledge, enhance their skills, and deepen their understanding of how we can all work together to make our communities better.

We wish you well, and we hope that you find the program a stimulating and valuable experience.

Sincerely,

Charles N. Quigley
EXECUTIVE DIRECTOR

ACKNOWLEDGEMENTS

Project Citizen Program Director
Michael Fischer

Curriculum Developers
Charles N. Quigley
Margaret Stimmann Branson
Roy Erickson
Duane E. Smith

Editorial Director
Theresa M. Richard

Associate Editor
David Hargrove

Production Editor
Mark Gage

Creative Director
Mark Stritzel

Illustrator
Richard Stein

Production Designer
Holly Small

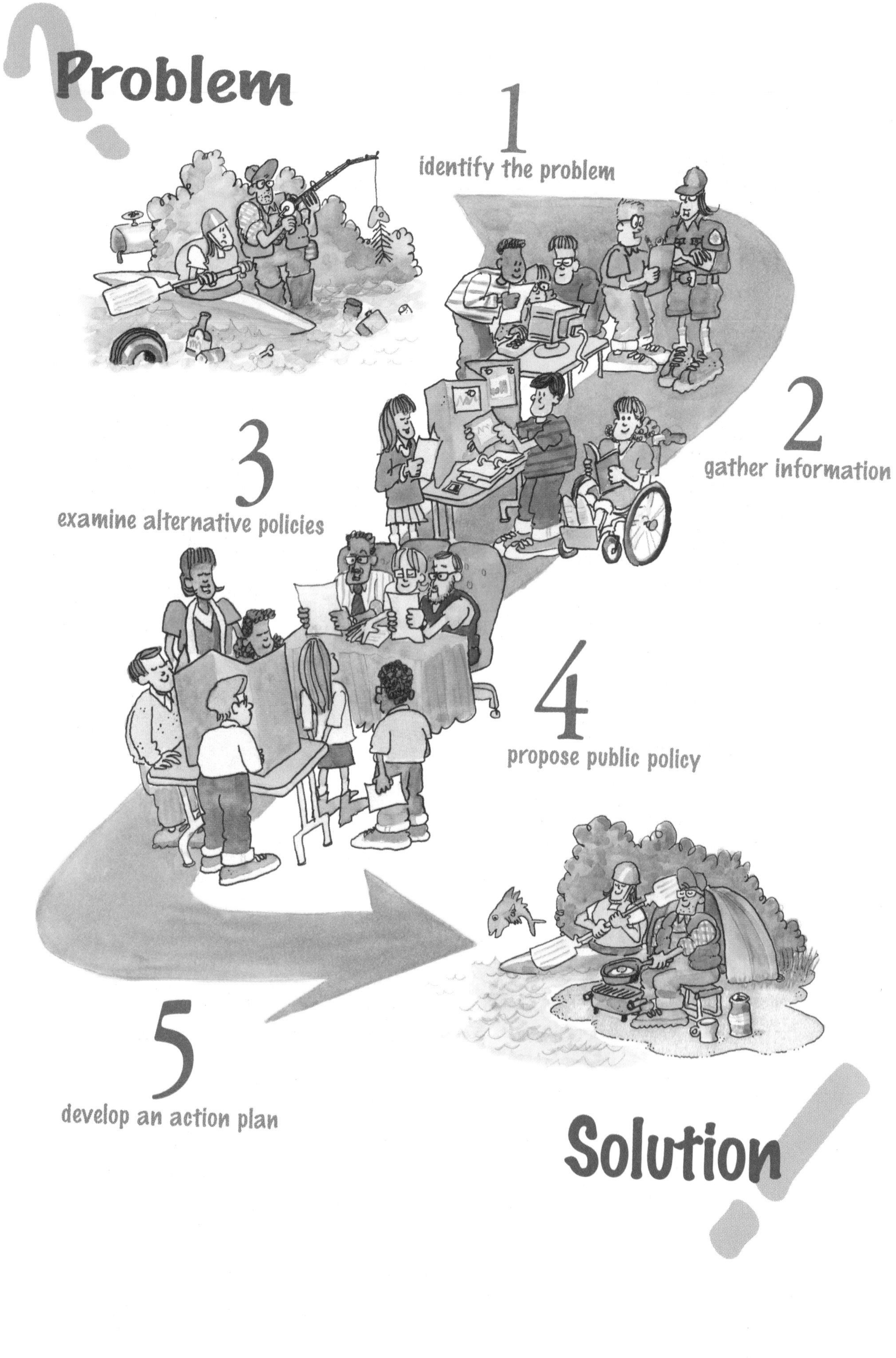

Problem

1

identify the problem

2

gather information

3

examine alternative policies

4

propose public policy

5

develop an action plan

Solution

INTRODUCTION

How Can Citizens Participate in Solving Community Problems?

In the United States a public policy is an agreed-upon way that our federal, state, or local government fulfills its responsibilities, such as protecting the rights of individuals and promoting the welfare of all the people. Some public policies are written into laws by legislatures. Other policies are contained in rules and regulations created by executive branches of government, the branches responsible for carrying out and enforcing laws.

The following are examples of public policies and the governmental agencies responsible for carrying them out:

- School districts are responsible for making policies regarding student behavior and discipline. Teachers and school administrators enforce these policies.
- State legislatures are responsible for making laws that place speed limits on drivers. Police officers enforce these laws.
- City governments often adopt policies that prohibit people from operating liquor stores near public schools. City inspectors and zoning departments enforce these policies.

When people become aware of problems in their communities, they often want government to develop and carry out policies to deal with those problems. These may be problems for which there are

- existing policies or laws that do not work well,
- existing policies or laws that are not being enforced,
- no policies or laws.

As a citizen of the United States you have a right to say what you think government should do about problems in your community. You also have a right to say what you think about problems in your state, the nation, and about international problems. You have the right to try to influence the decisions people in your government make about all of those problems.

To be able to participate effectively, however, citizens need to know which levels of government and which governmental agencies are responsible for changing, enforcing, or developing a specific public policy. For example, state legislatures may direct agencies to enact policies resulting from federal legislation, or local governments may create policies in order to carry out responsibilities assigned to them through laws enacted at the state or federal level. Additionally, as part of the process of developing and implementing policy, governmental agencies must determine if the new policy conflicts with existing legislation or policy.

This project is intended to help you learn how to express your opinions, how to decide which level of government and which agency is most appropriate for dealing with the problem you identify, and how to influence policy decisions at that level of government. It calls for you to work cooperatively with others in your class and with the help of your teacher and adult volunteers to accomplish the following tasks:

- **Identify a problem to study.**

  You will begin by identifying a problem in your community that you think is important and determine which level of government is most directly responsible for dealing with the problem.

- **Gather information.**

  When your class has decided on the problem you want to study, you will need to gather and evaluate information about the problem from a variety of sources.

- **Examine alternative policies.**

  Next, you will examine public policies that now are being used by your government. You also will examine policies being suggested by other people.

- **Propose and develop your own public policy.**

  Next, you will develop a public policy that you think your government should adopt.

- **Develop an action plan.**

  Finally, you will develop a plan of action to show how you might influence the appropriate government or governmental agency to adopt your proposed public policy.

Your class will use the materials you have gathered and written as you accomplish these tasks to develop a class portfolio. The portfolio is an organized collection of information that makes up your class plan related to a public policy issue that you and your class have decided to study.

The class portfolio will contain such things as written statements, charts, graphs, photographs, and original artwork. These materials will portray

1. what you have learned about the problem you have selected;
2. what you have learned about alternative solutions to the problem;
3. what public policy you have selected or developed to deal with the problem;
4. the plan of action you have developed to use in attempting to get your government to adopt your policy.

This instructional guide will provide step-by-step instructions for identifying and studying a public policy problem and for developing your class portfolio.

Your class is encouraged to present its portfolio orally to other classes in your school or to community groups. Your class may enter its portfolio in a showcase with other classes who have also developed portfolios.

The knowledge you gain in studying a problem in your community is valuable. It should be shared with others for their benefit. Sharing your knowledge and understanding also will benefit you. It will help you develop skills important for participation in a self-governing society. See Step 5: Presenting Your Portfolio, page 42–44, for more details on making oral presentations.

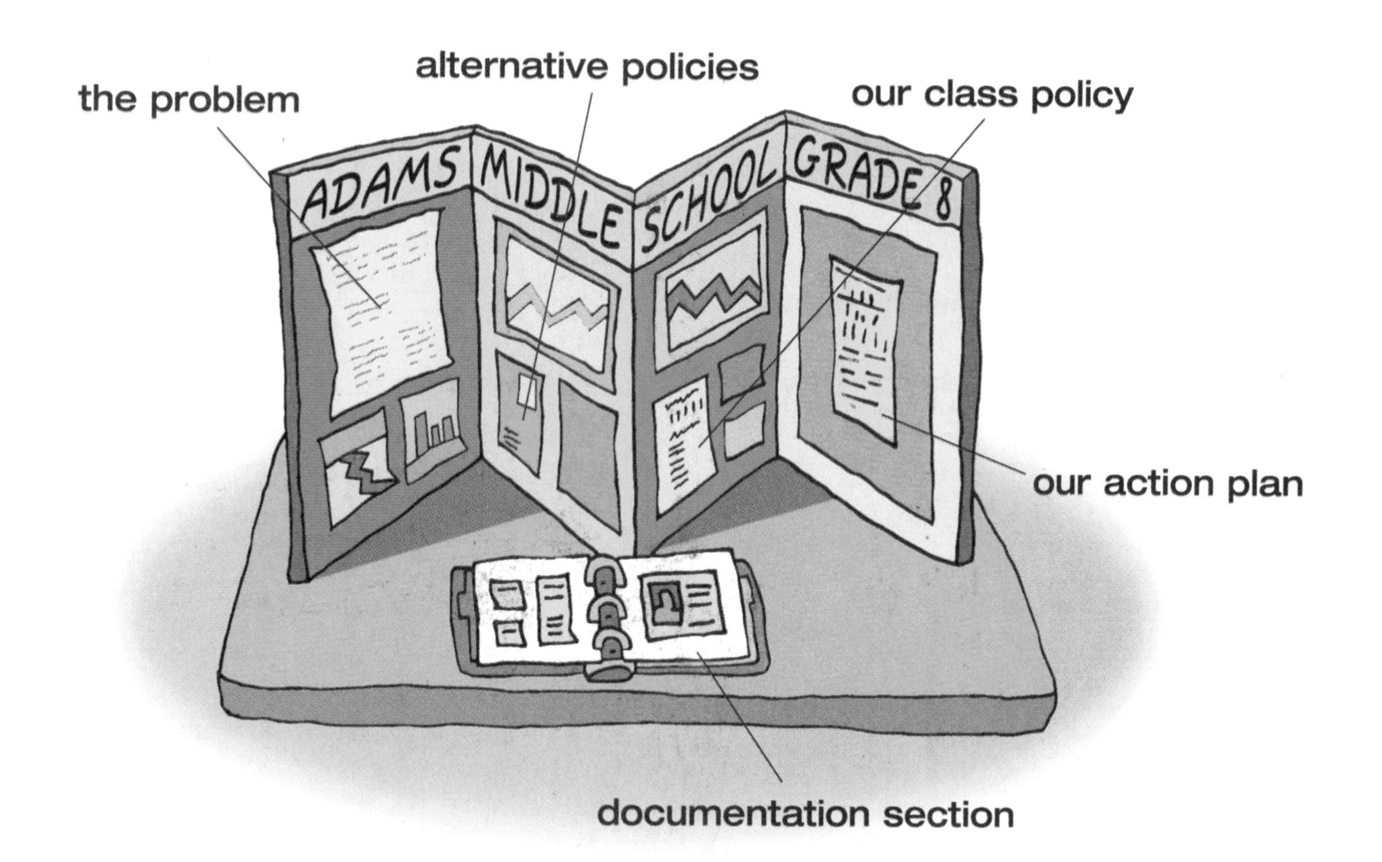

STEP 1

IDENTIFYING PUBLIC POLICY PROBLEMS IN YOUR COMMUNITY

PURPOSE

In this step you will read a short list of problems found in many communities in the United States. These represent problems people often think should be dealt with by their government. After reading the list, you will

- tell your class what you already know about these problems or what you have heard in discussions about them
- interview your parents and others in your community to learn and record what they know about these problems and their attitudes towards them

The purpose of this step is for you to share what you, your classmates, and others already know about problems in your community. This should help your class gain enough information to make an intelligent choice of one specific problem to study.

A CLASS DISCUSSION

Sharing what you know about problems in your community

To complete this activity, your entire class should

1. Read and discuss the problems listed on this page and page 5 that might be found in your community.
2. Divide into groups of two to three students. Each group should be assigned to discuss one of the problems. Then, the group should write its answers to the questions about the problem that are listed on the Problem Identification and Analysis Form on page 6.
3. Share each group's answers with the entire class.
4. Keep each group's completed forms for later use.

Common problems in communities

Communities across the United States have many problems in common. Some problems may be more serious in some communities than in others. People often think that government should be responsible for adopting policies to help solve these problems.

Problems in schools

1. Many people claim that schools do not teach skills that adequately prepare students to get jobs when they graduate.
2. Some students use language and other forms of expression that are insulting to certain groups.
3. Gang activity both in and out of school makes many students afraid for their personal safety.

B SMALL GROUP ACTIVITY

Problems regarding young people

1. Young people sometimes work long hours in after-school or weekend jobs. This often makes it difficult for them to do well in school.

2. Some working parents do not have enough money to pay for adequate child-care during working hours. As a result, young children may be left home alone, sometimes in dangerous circumstances.

Problems involving community standards

1. Some stores advertise and sell tobacco and alcohol near schools. Others sell materials that some people might think obscene near schools.

2. Some facilities or group homes for elderly persons or persons with disabilities do not meet health or safety standards. Some may treat residents poorly.

Problems involving basic liberties

1. Large numbers of people do not vote in elections. This is especially true in local elections.

2. Many people argue that money plays too great a role in the election of government officials.

Problems concerning the environment

1. Some communities have problems that involve conflicts about the protection of the environment and the protection of jobs.

2. Some communities do not have recycling programs or those they have do not work well.

Work with one or two other students to discuss the problem you have been assigned. Then write your answers to the questions on the Problem Identification and Analysis Form on page 6.

If your class wishes to investigate a problem not listed, it may do so.

PROBLEM IDENTIFICATION AND ANALYSIS FORM

Names of group members ____________________
Date ____________________
The problem ____________________

1. Is this a problem that you and other people in your community think is important? Why?

2. What level of government or governmental agency is responsible for dealing with the problem?

3. What policy, if any, does government now have to deal with this problem?

   If a policy does exist, answer the following questions:

   - What are its advantages and disadvantages?
   - How might it be improved?
   - Does this policy need to be replaced? Why?
   - What disagreements, if any, exist in your community about this policy?

4. Where can you get more information about this problem and the positions taken by different individuals and groups?

5. Are there other problems in your community that you think might be useful for your class to study? What are they?

C HOMEWORK ASSIGNMENTS

Finding out more about problems in your community

The three assignments that follow should help you learn more about problems in your community and the public policies designed to deal with them. Use the forms provided to record the information you gather. Save all the information you collect during these assignments. You may want to include some of it in your class portfolio.

1. **Interview Assignment**
   Select one problem from the suggestions on pages 4 and 5 or a problem your class has identified. Discuss the problem with your family, friends, neighbors, or others. Find out what they know about the problem in your community and how they feel about it. Use the Interview Form on page 8 to record the information you receive.

2. **Printed Sources Assignment**
   Look in newspapers and other printed sources of information for evidence of the problem and policies designed to deal with it in your community. Bring materials you find to your class. Share them with your teacher and your classmates. Use the Printed Sources Form on page 9 to record the printed information you have looked at.

3. **Radio, TV, and Internet Assignment**
   Look or listen for news reports and other information on the radio, television, or the Internet concerning the problem and related policies. Bring the information to class to share with your teacher and other classmates. Use the Radio/Television/Internet Sources Form on page 10 to record the information you have gathered.

INTERVIEW FORM

Your name ______________________________

Date ______________________________

The problem ______________________________

1. Name of person interviewed ______________________________

   Note: If a person does not wish to be named, respect his or her privacy and indicate only the person's role in the community (e.g., business person, retired person, parent, student, community volunteer).

2. Tell the person which problem you are studying. Then ask the following questions. Record the answers you receive.

   a. Is this a problem that you think is important? Why?

   ____

   ____

   b. Do you think others in our community believe this is an important problem? Why?

   ____

   ____

   c. What policy, if any, does government now have to deal with this problem?

   ____

   ____

   If a policy does exist answer the following questions:

   - What are the advantages of this policy?

     ____

     ____

   - What are the disadvantages of this policy?

     ____

     ____

   - How might the policy be improved?

     ____

     ____

   - Does it need to be replaced? Why?

     ____

     ____

   - What disagreements about this policy, if any, exist in our community?

     ____

     ____

   d. Where can I (or my class) get more information about this problem and the different positions people take on the problem.

   ____

   ____

PRINTED SOURCES FORM

Your name ______________________

Date ______________________

The problem ______________________

Name/date of publication ______________________

Title of the article ______________________

1. Position taken in the article related to problem

____

____

2. Main points of the position

____

____

____

____

____

3. According to the source what policy, if any, does government now have to deal with this problem?

____

____

If a policy does exist answer the following questions:

- What are the advantages of this policy?

  ____

  ____

- What are the disadvantages of this policy?

  ____

  ____

- How might the policy be improved?

  ____

  ____

  ____

- Does it need to be replaced? Why?

  ____

  ____

  ____

- What disagreements about this policy, if any, exist in our community?

  ____

  ____

  ____

  ____

RADIO/TELEVISION/INTERNET SOURCES FORM

Your name ______________________________

Date ____________________ Time ____________________

The problem ______________________________

1. Source of information ______________________________
   (This might be a website, television or radio news program, documentary, interview show, or some other program that addresses the problem.)

   Consider the following questions as you gather information from your sources:

2. Is this a problem that is thought to be important? Why?

3. What policy, if any, does government now have to deal with this problem?

   If a policy does exist answer the following questions:

   - What are the advantages of this policy?
   - What are the disadvantages of this policy?
   - How might the policy be improved?
   - Does it need to be replaced? Why?
   - What disagreements about this policy, if any, exist in our community?

STEP 2

SELECTING A PROBLEM FOR CLASS STUDY

PURPOSE

Your entire class should discuss what you have discovered about the problems in your community. Decide if you have enough information to select a problem for class study.

A CLASS DISCUSSION

Deciding if you have enough information to select a problem

Use the following steps to select one specific problem for your class to study:

1. If your class thinks it has enough information to make a decision, the class should select a problem by majority vote. Be sure to select a problem that is important to you and your community. Be sure that it is a problem about which you can gather information to develop a good portfolio.
2. If your class decides it needs more information before making a decision on which problem to study, homework assignments may be given to different groups to gather more information on the problems.

STEP 3

GATHERING INFORMATION ON THE PROBLEM YOUR CLASS WILL STUDY

PURPOSE

Now that your class has selected a problem, you must decide where to get additional information. You will find that some sources of information will be better than others. For example, if you have selected an environmental problem, you will find that certain individuals and groups know more about that problem in your community than others.

A CLASS DISCUSSION

Identifying sources of information

The following is a list of some sources of information you might explore. Read and discuss the list. Decide which sources to contact. Then divide into research teams.

Each research team should gather information from one of the sources listed or others your class identifies. Forms to use in gathering and recording information are included on pages 8–10 and 17–20. Refer to the appendices on pages 49–50 for examples of sources of information and how to contact them.

Adult volunteers may assist your team in gathering information, but they should not do your work for you. Save all the information you gather for use in the development of the class portfolio.

You might wish to invite people to visit your class to share what they know about the problem you are studying.

Examples of sources of information

1. **Libraries**

   School, public, college, and university libraries in your community have newspapers and other publications with information about the problem you are researching. Librarians are there to help you find the information you need. Libraries may have coin-operated machines for making photocopies of the information you may wish to use in your portfolio.

2. **Newspaper Offices**

   You may wish to contact the offices of newspapers in your community. Newspaper reporters gather information on problems in their communities and what government is doing about them. Newspaper offices and reporters may be able to provide your class with clippings on the problem you are studying. They can also provide photographs for which they may charge a small fee.

3. **Professors and Scholars**

   Professors in local colleges or universities may be experts on the problem you are studying. Your phone book will list the public information offices of nearby colleges and universities. You can call those offices for help in locating scholars who might be helpful. You also could contact high school teachers of government in your community.

4. **Lawyers or Judges**

   Most lawyers and judges belong to bar associations that provide some free services to the public. Both lawyers and judges are excellent sources of information on many problems in communities. Ask the principal if there are parents of students at your school who are lawyers. Use a telephone directory to find the bar association nearest you.

5. **Community Organizations and Interest Groups**

   Many groups take an interest in problems found in our communities and the nation. These are called interest groups. Some may be found in your community or area. Use a telephone directory to find their offices. Your class may have identified some interest groups dealing with the problem you are studying when you did the first homework assignment. Your teacher or an adult volunteer can help you call or write to them for information.

6. **Legislative Offices**

Your representatives in the legislative or law-making branches of your local government, state government, and the United States Congress are responsible for identifying problems and suggesting or supporting public policies to deal with them.

Your member of Congress and your representative in your state's legislature each has an office in your community, area, or state. You can find the address and phone numbers of these offices in a telephone book. Each office will have one or more people on its staff responsible for helping you and other citizens gain information about problems in your community, state, or the nation.

Members of Congress may be able to obtain briefing papers on the problem you are studying from the Congressional Research Service, a part of the Library of Congress.

7. **Administrative Agencies**

People working in the administrative agencies of your local, state, and national government may deal with the problem your class has chosen to study. Public information offices can provide information on the problem and what the government is doing about it. For example, your local government may have a health department or a building safety department. Use your phone book to find these or other appropriate offices.

8. **Internet**

Many of the above sources as well as numerous others are available online through the Internet. If your school does not have access to the Internet, check with libraries in your area.

B GUIDELINES

For Obtaining and Documenting Information

Most people working in the places where you can find information are very busy people. It is important to follow the suggestions given below to avoid having the class place too much of a burden on the offices and individuals being asked for information.

1. **Visiting libraries and other places where information can be found**
   Individually or in small groups you may visit libraries or offices of various public and private groups that have information on the problem. (Use the Information from Print or Electronic Sources Form on pages 17 and 18.)

2. **Calling sources on the phone**
   No more than one student should be given the assignment of calling any office for information. It is important, therefore, that the student who calls clearly records the information gained during a phone interview. (Use the Information from Letters or Interviews–Documentation Form on pages 19 and 20 to record the information you receive.)

3. **Making appointments and interviewing people**
   One student should call to arrange for an appointment. A small group may visit an office or person to conduct a personal interview. (Use the Information from Letters or Interviews–Documentation Form on pages 19 and 20 to record the information you receive.)

4. **Writing and requesting information**
   One or more students may write a letter requesting information from each office or person. Including a self-addressed stamped envelope may help you get a response. (Use the Information from Letters or Interviews–Documentation Form on pages 19 and 20 to record the information you receive.)

C HOMEWORK ASSIGNMENT

Researching the problem in your community

After deciding what sources of information to use, your class should be divided into research teams. Each team should be responsible for gathering information from a different source.

If you are the person in your research team who is assigned to contact one of the sources of information described on pages 12–14, begin by introducing yourself. Then inform the person of your purpose or why you are contacting him or her. Use the following guidelines for introducing yourself by letter or in person.

Use the Information from Letters or Interviews–Documentation Form on pages 19 and 20 to record the answers you receive.

Introducing Yourself

My name is [your name]. I am a student in [teacher's name] [your grade] class in [name of school].

We are studying local problems, how they are dealt with by government, and how citizens can participate in their government.

The problem my class is studying is [briefly describe the problem].

I am responsible for finding out information about the problem to share with my class.

May I ask you a few questions now or is there another time that would be better for me to call? Is there another person I should call?

Do you have any printed information on the problem that you can send us? [If you are calling on the phone and the answer is yes, be prepared to give the person the address of your school.]

INFORMATION FROM PRINT OR ELECTRONIC SOURCES FORM

Name(s) of research team member(s) ____________________

Date ____________________

The problem being researched ____________________

Name of library, office, agency, or website visited ____________________

1. Source of information ____________________

   a. Name of publication/website ____________________

   b. Author (if noted) ____________________

   c. Date of publication/website ____________________

2. Record information from the publication or website that helps you answer as many of the following questions as you can.

   a. How serious is this problem in our community?

   ____

   ____

   ____

   b. How widespread is the problem in our state or nation?

   ____

   ____

   ____

   c. Which of the following do you think is true?

   - There is no law or policy for dealing with the problem. ❑ Yes ❑ No
   - The law for dealing with the problem is not adequate. ❑ Yes ❑ No
   - The law for dealing with the problem is adequate, but it is not being well enforced. ❑ Yes ❑ No

   d. What levels of government or governmental agencies, if any, are responsible for dealing with the problem? What are they doing about the problem?

   ____

   ____

   ____

   ____

   e. What disagreements about this policy or ways of dealing with it exist in our community?

   ____

   ____

   ____

   ____

   ____

   ____

   ____

INFORMATION FROM PRINT OR ELECTRONIC SOURCES FORM

f. Who are the major individuals, groups, or organizations expressing opinions on the problem?

- Why are they interested in the problem?

- What positions are they taking?

- What are the advantages and disadvantages of their positions?

- How are they trying to influence government to adopt their position on the problem?

g. How can my classmates and I get more information on their positions?

INFORMATION FROM LETTERS OR INTERVIEWS – DOCUMENTATION FORM

Name(s) of research team member(s) ____________________

Date ____________________

The problem being researched ____________________

1. Source of information

   a. Name ____________________

   b. Title and organization ____________________

   c. Address ____________________

   d. Phone ____________________

2. Request information about the problem. After introducing yourself by letter or phone as suggested on page 16, ask for answers to the following questions.

   a. How serious is this problem in our community?

   ____

   ____

   ____

   ____

   b. How widespread is the problem in our state or nation?

   ____

   ____

   ____

   ____

   c. Why is this a problem that should be handled by government? Should anyone else also take responsibility for solving the problem? Why?

   ____

   ____

   ____

   d. Which of the following do you think is true?

   - There is no law or policy for dealing with the problem. ❑ Yes ❑ No
   - The law for dealing with the problem is not adequate. ❑ Yes ❑ No
   - The law for dealing with the problem is adequate, but it is not being well enforced. ❑ Yes ❑ No

   e. What levels of government or governmental agencies, if any, are responsible for dealing with the problem? What are they doing about the problem?

   ____

   ____

   ____

   ____

INFORMATION FROM LETTERS OR INTERVIEWS - DOCUMENTATION FORM (CONTINUED)

f. What disagreements about this policy or ways of dealing with it exist in our community?

____
____
____
____

g. Who are the major individuals, groups, or organizations expressing opinions on the problem?

____
____
____
____

- Why are they interested in the problem?

  ____
  ____
  ____

- What positions are they taking?

  ____
  ____
  ____

- What are the advantages and disadvantages of their positions?

  ____
  ____
  ____

- How can we get information on their positions?

  ____
  ____
  ____

- How are they trying to influence government to adopt their positions on the problem?

  ____
  ____
  ____

h. If our class develops a policy to deal with this problem,
how might we influence our government to adopt our policy?

____
____
____
____
____
____
____
____

STEP 4

DEVELOPING A CLASS PORTFOLIO

PURPOSE

You should now have completed enough research to begin to develop your class portfolio. First your class will need to work together to discuss and answer questions on a series of worksheets that will be used to guide the development of your portfolio. Next, the class should be divided into four groups. Each group will be responsible for developing one part of the portfolio.

The materials in the portfolios should include the best documentation the class and group have gathered in investigating the problem. It also should include students' original written materials and/or artwork.

A WORKSHEETS

Reaching a Common Understanding and Agreement

To help you understand what needs to be done to successfully complete each of the four portfolio tasks, everyone in your class will work together to complete the following worksheets. When the class is satisfied with their answers, your teacher will either assign you to one of the four portfolio task groups, or ask you to select a group.

After the class has finished discussing the worksheets, use them to guide the development of your part of the portfolio – both the display board and documentation binder. As you work on your portfolio task you should communicate with the other task groups to share your information and report on your progress.

Molly McKenna

TASK ONE - EXPLAINING THE PROBLEM

The first thing you and your classmates will need to do is to clearly explain the problem you have chosen. You will need to explain why the problem is important, which individuals or groups in the community are interested in this problem, and which part of government has responsibility for dealing with it. To accomplish this you will need to answer the following questions:

1. What is the problem that you and your classmates want to study?

   Easy access to M-Rated games and movies. (youth)

2. How serious is this problem in your community?

   We think this is a serious problem, based on our research and knowledge.

3. How widespread is this problem in your community?

   It's too easy for youth to get videos. It's pretty widespread. It's also easy that it doesn't matter whether video or game or department store. It's still easy to get.

4. Why is it a problem that should be handled by government?

   It's leading to crime, so yes, the government should handle it.

5. Should anyone else in the community take responsibility for solving the problem?

   yes. the stores should take some of the responsibility, also the parents.

6. Is there an existing law or policy for dealing with the problem?

   there is an existing law or policy for dealing with the problem. Individual Stores have exsisting polocies.

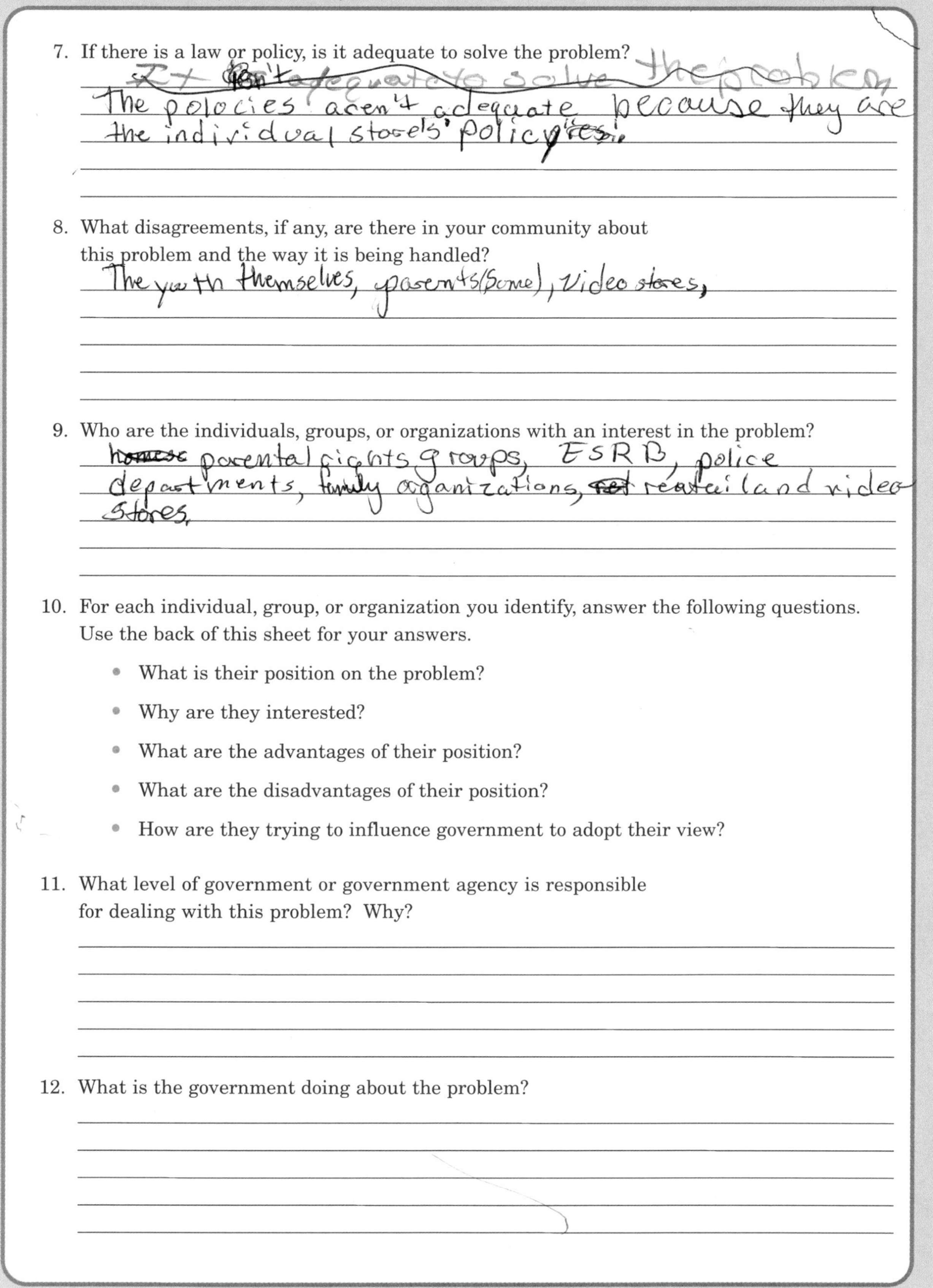

7. If there is a law or policy, is it adequate to solve the problem?

   The polocies aren't adequate because they are the individual stores' policies.

8. What disagreements, if any, are there in your community about this problem and the way it is being handled?

   The youth themselves, parents(Some), Video stores,

9. Who are the individuals, groups, or organizations with an interest in the problem?

   parental rights groups, ESRB, police departments, family organizations, reatail and video stores,

10. For each individual, group, or organization you identify, answer the following questions. Use the back of this sheet for your answers.

    - What is their position on the problem?
    - Why are they interested?
    - What are the advantages of their position?
    - What are the disadvantages of their position?
    - How are they trying to influence government to adopt their view?

11. What level of government or government agency is responsible for dealing with this problem? Why?

12. What is the government doing about the problem?

TASK TWO - EXAMINING ALTERNATIVE POLICIES

You must identify several alternative policies for dealing with the problem you have chosen. These policies may include an existing policy or policies being proposed by individuals or groups in the community. You should also include your own original ideas for policies to address the problem.

For each policy presented you should

1. State the policy or suggested policy
2. Identify the individual or group that is proposing the policy
   (this could be your own class or group)
3. Identify the advantages of this proposed policy
4. Identify the disadvantages of this proposed policy
5. Identify other individuals or groups in the community who are likely to support this policy
6. Identify other individuals or groups in the community who are likely to oppose this policy

Use the bottom and back of this page to write your answers for each policy you identify.

TASK THREE - PROPOSING A PUBLIC POLICY

Next, you will need to propose a public policy to deal with the problem. It must not violate the U.S. Constitution or your state's constitution. It may be one of the alternative policies you discussed earlier, a modification of one of those policies, or it may be your own original idea. Answer the questions below and complete the Constitutional Opinion Form on pages 36–37.

1. We think the best public policy to deal with this problem is

____
____
____
____
____
____

2. The advantages of this policy are

____
____
____
____
____
____

3. The disadvantages of this policy are

____
____
____
____
____
____

4. Identify the level of government that would be responsible for carrying out your proposed policy. Explain why this level of government is responsible.

____
____
____
____
____

5. The policy being proposed is constitutional because (Use your answers from the Constitutional Opinion Form to complete this item.)

____
____
____
____
____
____
____

TASK FOUR – DEVELOPING AN ACTION PLAN

You will need to develop an action plan to get your policy adopted by the appropriate governmental body or agency. This plan should include the steps you will need to take to get your proposed policy enacted and implemented by the government.

1. The main activities of our plan are

2. Influential individuals and groups who might be willing to support our proposed policy are

3. To win their support we can

4. Influential individuals and groups who might oppose our proposed policy are

5. We might be able to win some support from these individuals and groups by

6. Influential government officials and/or agencies that might be willing to support our proposed policy are

7. We can gain their support by

8. Influential government officials and/or agencies that might oppose our policy are

9. We might be able to gain their support by

B GROUP TASKS

The following are the tasks of each portfolio group. Each group should select from the materials gathered by all the research teams those that help them complete the tasks described below. (More detailed instructions for each group are included in section D.)

Portfolio Group One: Explaining the problem

This group is responsible for explaining the problem that the class has chosen to study. The group also should explain why the problem is important and why that level of government or governmental agency should deal with it.

Portfolio Group Two: Examining alternative policies to deal with the problem

This group is responsible for explaining present and/or alternative policies designed to solve the problem.

Portfolio Group Three: Proposing a public policy to deal with the problem

This group is responsible for developing and justifying a specific public policy that the majority of the class agrees to support.

Portfolio Group Four: Developing an action plan

This group is responsible for developing an action plan showing how citizens can influence their government to adopt the policy the class supports.

C EVALUATION CRITERIA

On pages 40–41 there is a Portfolio Criteria Checklist that will help you develop the best possible portfolio. You will also need to refer to the specific requirements for the display and documentation sections for each of the Portfolio Groups to be sure you have included everything that is expected. You can find these specifics in the description of the each group's task on pages 30–39. Use this information as a guide while you are developing your portfolio.

You should also think about the overall effect your portfolio will have on someone who reads it. You will want the portfolio to show creative problem solving and originality. Be careful to select the best information you have gathered to include in the display or in the binder.

If your class enters its portfolio in a showcase with other classes, a panel of evaluators will consider the Portfolio Criteria Checklist as they evaluate your portfolio. They will give separate ratings to each of your portfolio sections and to the portfolio as a whole.

D GROUP INSTRUCTIONS

The instructions on pages 30–39 specify each group's tasks in more detail. Although each group has specific tasks, it is important that they communicate with one another to share ideas and information. Each group should keep the entire class informed of its progress and work cooperatively with the other groups so that the class develops the best portfolio it can.

Groups should collaborate as they decide what specific items should be included in the display and documentation sections of the portfolio. This collaboration will avoid displaying the same information more than once and guarantee the inclusion of the best exhibits or evidence.

E SPECIFICATIONS

The work of all four groups will be featured in a class portfolio. It will have two sections: a display section and a documentation section.

1. **Display section**
   For this section the work of each of the four groups should be placed on a separate panel of the four-panel display. The display should be composed of four sheets of poster board or foam-core board, or the equivalent, no larger than 32" wide by 40" high. The display should be developed so it can be placed on a table, bulletin board, or an easel. Materials to be displayed may include written statements, a list of sources, charts, graphs, photographs, original art work, etc. (See the illustration on page 3.)

2. **Documentation section**
   Each of the four groups should select from the materials gathered those that best document or give evidence of their research. Materials included in the documentation section should represent samples of the most important and/or significant research you have completed. Not all research should be included.

   Documentation materials should be put in a three-ring binder no larger than 2" thick. Use different colored dividers to separate the four sections. Prepare a table of contents for each section.

PORTFOLIO GROUP 1

EXPLAINING THE PROBLEM

Your group is responsible for explaining the problem in the first display and documentation sections of your class portfolio.

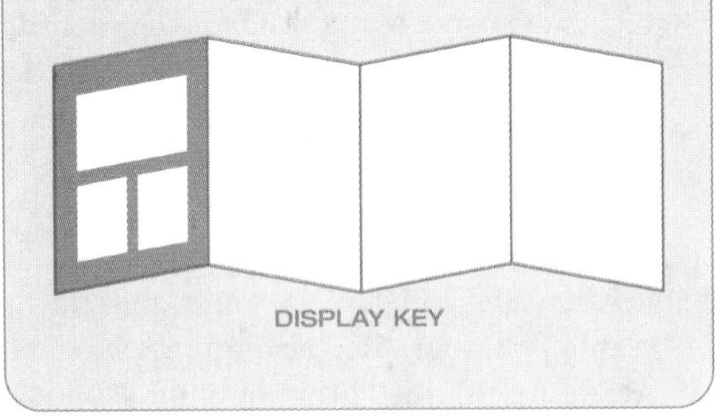

DISPLAY KEY

A DISPLAY SECTION : PART 1

This part should include the following items:

1. **A written summary of the problem**
   Review material gathered by research teams. Write no more than two double-spaced typed pages explaining the problem. Summarize what you have learned about the problem using the answers your class developed on the Task One–Explaining the Problem worksheet (pages 22–23).

2. **Graphic presentations of the problem**
   This may include charts, graphs, photos, political cartoons, newspaper headlines, tables of statistics, and other illustrations. Illustrations may be from printed sources or they may be your original creations. Each illustration should have a caption or title.

3. **Identification of your sources of information**
   On one or more typed pages, identify sources the class has used.

B DOCUMENTATION SECTION : PART 1

In Part 1 of the class binder include copies of the best or most important information your class gathered and used in your examination and explanation of the problem. For example, you may include selected

- newspaper or magazine clippings,
- written reports of interviews with people in the community,
- written reports of radio and television coverage of the problem,
- communications from public and private interest groups, and
- excerpts from government publications.

Lengthy documents and reports should be represented by copies of their title pages, tables of content, and a one-page summary (or abstract) of the document either taken from the document itself or written by the group. Be sure to prepare a table of contents for this section.

PORTFOLIO GROUP 2

EXAMINING ALTERNATIVE POLICIES TO DEAL WITH THE PROBLEM

Your group is responsible for clearly explaining and evaluating present and/or alternative policies designed to deal with the problem. Your findings are presented in the second display and documentation sections of your class portfolio.

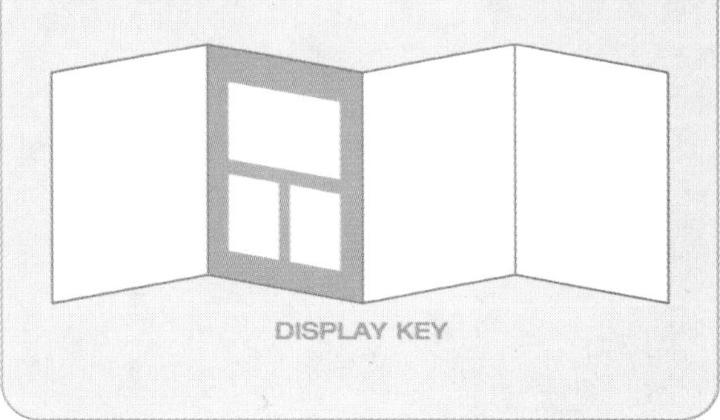

DISPLAY KEY

A DISPLAY SECTION : PART 2

This part should include the following items:

1. **A written summary of alternative policies**
   Select two or three of the policies proposed by different individuals or groups. (You may include an existing policy.) Refer to the ideas your class developed when you completed the Task Two–Examining Alternative Policies worksheet (page 24) to guide your work on this section of the portfolio.

2. **Graphic presentations of the policies**
   This may include charts, graphs, photos, drawings, political cartoons, newspaper headlines, tables of statistics, and other illustrations related to the policies. These illustrations may come from printed sources or they may be your original creations. Each illustration should have a caption or title.

3. **Identification of your sources of information**
   On one or more typed pages, identify sources the class has used to gather information.

B DOCUMENTATION SECTION : PART 2

Include in Part 2 of the class binder copies of the best or most important information your class gathered and used in examining and evaluating present and alternative policies to deal with the problem. For example, you may include as documentation selected

- newspaper or magazine clippings,
- written reports or summaries of interviews with people in the community,
- written reports of radio and television coverage of the problem,
- communications from public and private interest groups, and
- excerpts from government publications.

Lengthy documents and reports should be represented by copies of their title pages, tables of content, and a one-page summary (or abstract) of the document either taken from the document itself or written by the group. Be sure to prepare a table of contents for this section.

PORTFOLIO GROUP 3

PROPOSING A PUBLIC POLICY TO DEAL WITH THE PROBLEM

Your group is responsible for proposing a public policy to deal with the problem. The policy your group chooses must be agreed to by a majority of your class. It must also be a policy that does not violate the U.S. Constitution or your state constitution. A Constitutional Opinion Form is included on pages 36–37 to assist you and your class. Once this is decided your class may choose to

- support one of the alternative policies identified by Portfolio Group 2,
- modify one of those policies, or
- develop your own policy.

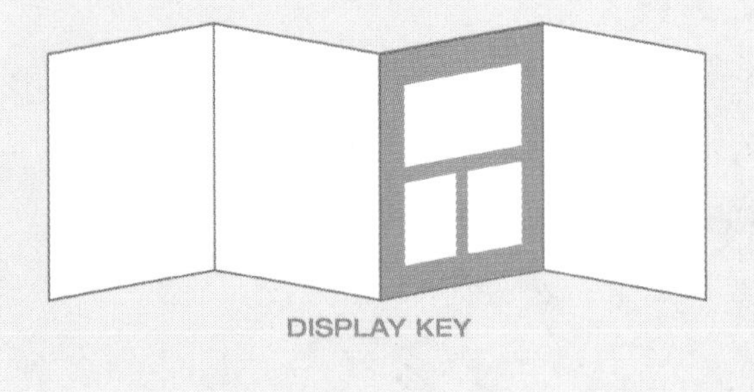

DISPLAY KEY

A DISPLAY SECTION : PART 3

This part should include the following items:

1. **A written explanation and justification for your suggested policy**
   You should explain in no more than two, double-spaced pages, the policy your class selects and your reasons for supporting it. Refer to the proposed policy your class developed when you completed the Task Three – Proposing a Public Policy worksheet (page 25) to guide your work on this section of the portfolio.

2. **Graphic presentations of your proposed policy**
   This may include charts, graphs, photos, drawings, political cartoons, newspaper headlines, tables of statistics, and other illustrations related to the policy and the problem it is designed to solve. These illustrations may come from printed sources or they may be your original creations. Each illustration should have a caption or title.

3. **Identification of your sources of information**
   On one or more typed pages, identify sources the class has used to gather information.

B DOCUMENTATION SECTION : PART 3

Include in Part 3 of the class binder copies of the best or most important information your class gathered and used in developing its proposed policy. For example, you may include as documentation selected

- newspaper or magazine clippings,
- written reports or summaries of interviews with people in the community,
- written reports of radio and television coverage of the problem,
- communications from public and private interest groups, and
- excerpts from government publications.

Lengthy documents and reports should be represented by copies of their title pages, tables of content, and a one-page summary (or abstract) of the document either taken from the document itself or written by the group. Be sure to include a table of contents for this section.

CONSTITUTIONAL OPINION FORM

The United States Constitution and Bill of Rights place limits on what government can do in order to protect the rights of the people. So do the constitutions of each state.

Whenever we suggest that government adopt a policy or enact a law to deal with a problem, it is important that we do not ask government to do something prohibited by our federal or state constitutions. Each citizen has the right and should take the responsibility to look at present and suggested policies and laws to see if they might be violating constitutional limits on government.

This checklist includes some of the most important limits our federal and state constitutions place on our governments to protect our rights. Use the checklist when you develop your policy. Be sure that, in your opinion, your proposed policy does not violate the limits placed on government.

This Constitutional Opinion Form should be considered by the entire class. The results of that consideration should be included in Part 3 of the display and documentation sections of your portfolio.

Checklist

1. Government is not allowed to interfere with a person's freedom of belief. Our proposed policy (does/does not) violate this limit on the power of government. Explain why.

____
____
____
____
____
____

2. Government is not allowed to place unreasonable and unfair limits on a person's right to express himself or herself in speech, writing, or by other means. Our proposed policy (does/does not) violate this limit on the power of government. Explain why.

____
____
____
____
____
____

3. Government is not allowed to take a person's life, liberty, or property without giving that person a fair hearing in a court of law or before another authorized agency of government. Our proposed policy (does/does not) violate this limit on the power of government. Explain why.

____
____
____
____
____
____

4. Government is not allowed to invade the privacy of a person's home without a very good reason for doing so. Our proposed policy (does/does not) violate this limit on the power of government. Explain why.

5. Government is not allowed to make laws that unreasonably or unfairly discriminate against people on the basis of race, religion, age, ethnic group (national origin), or gender. Our proposed policy (does/does not) violate this limit on the power of government. Explain why.

Summary Statement

Write a summary statement in which you support your belief that your class's proposed public policy does not violate the U.S. Constitution or your state's constitution.

PORTFOLIO GROUP 4

DEVELOPING AN ACTION PLAN

Your group is responsible for developing a plan of action. The plan should include steps you might take to get your proposed policy accepted and implemented by government. Your entire class should be involved in developing the plan, but your group will explain the plan in Part 4 of the display section and Part 4 of the documentation section of your class portfolio.

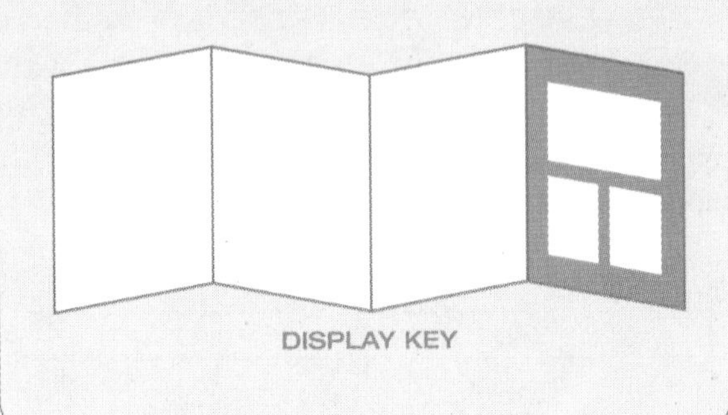

DISPLAY KEY

A DISPLAY SECTION : PART 4

This part should include the following items:

1. **A written explanation of how your class could develop support among individuals and groups in your community for your proposed plan**
   As your group works on this section of the portfolio, refer to the ideas developed by the class when you completed the Task Four – Developing an Action Plan worksheet (pages 26–27). On one double-spaced typed page, describe the main points of your plan.

2. **A written explanation of how your class could develop support by your government for your proposed policy**
   On one double-spaced typed page, describe the main points of your plan.

3. **Graphic presentations of your action plan**
   This may include charts, graphs, photos, drawings, political cartoons, newspaper headlines, tables of statistics, and other illustrations. These illustrations may come from printed sources or they may be your original creations. Each illustration should have a caption or title.

4. **Identification of your sources of information**
   On one or more typed pages, identify sources the class has used to gather information.

B DOCUMENTATION SECTION : PART 4

Include in Part 4 of the class binder copies of the best or most important information your class gathered and used in developing your action plan. For example, you may include as documentation selected

- statements by influential individuals and groups,
- statements by influential government officials and agencies,
- newspaper or magazine clippings,
- written reports of interviews with people in the community,
- written reports of radio and television coverage of the problem,
- communications from public and private interest groups, and
- excerpts from government publications.

Lengthy documents and reports should be represented by copies of their title pages, tables of content, and a one-page summary (or abstract) of the document either taken from the document itself or written by the group.

PORTFOLIO CRITERIA CHECKLIST - EACH SECTION

❏ **Completeness**

- Does each section include the material described on pages 30–39 for Portfolio Groups 1–4?
- Have you included more than you need?

❏ **Clarity**

- Is your portfolio well organized?
- Is your portfolio clearly written, grammatical, and correctly spelled?
- Are major points and arguments easy to understand?

❏ **Information**

- Is the information accurate?
- Does the information cover major facts and important concepts?
- Is the information you included important for understanding your topic?

❏ **Support**

- Have you given examples to explain or support your major points?
- Have you given thoughtful explanations for your major points?

❏ **Graphics**

- Do your graphics relate specifically to your section's content?
- Do your graphics provide information?
- Does each have a caption or title?
- Do your graphics help people understand your display?

❏ **Documentation**

- Have you documented the major points in your portfolio section?
- Have you used reliable, trustworthy, and varied sources?
- If you quoted or paraphrased your sources of information, do you give them credit each time?
- Does your documentation clearly relate to the display?
- Have you selected only the best and most important sources of information?

❏ **Constitutionality**

- Have you included your Constitutional Opinion Form?
- Have you explained why your proposed policy does not violate the Constitution?

PORTFOLIO CRITERIA CHECKLIST - OVERALL PORTFOLIO

❑ **Persuasiveness**

- Does your portfolio give ample evidence that your selected problem is important?
- Does your proposed policy address the problem directly?
- Does your portfolio explain how you might gain public support for the proposed policy?

❑ **Practicality**

- Is your proposed policy practical and realistic?
- Is your plan for gaining support for your proposed policy realistic?

❑ **Coordination**

- Does each of the four parts of your display portfolio relate to the others without repeating information?
- Does the documentation section of your portfolio provide evidence to support your display portfolio?

❑ **Reflection**

- Does the section where you reflect on and evaluate the development of your portfolio demonstrate that you have thought carefully about your experience?
- Do you demonstrate what you have learned from the portfolio development experience?

STEP 5

PRESENTING YOUR PORTFOLIO

PURPOSE

When your class portfolio is completed, you can present your project before an audience. Your presentation can be made to a three- or four-person panel representing your school and community. These panel members will evaluate your presentation based on the same criteria you used to develop your portfolio. This activity will give you valuable experience in presenting important ideas to others and convincing them of your position.

DISPLAY KEY

GOALS

There are four basic goals of the presentation:

1. To **inform** an audience of the importance of the problem identified in your community.
2. To **explain and evaluate** alternative polices so that an audience can understand the advantages and disadvantages of each.
3. To **discuss** your class's choice as the best policy to deal with the problem and make the case for that policy. To make and support your class's view that the proposed policy does not violate the federal and your state's constitution.
4. To **demonstrate** how your class could develop support for its policy in your community, as well as in the legislative and executive branches of the appropriate level of government.

Each of these goals matches the four groups that had responsibility for your portfolio display. During the presentation each of the four portfolio groups will have an opportunity to present its work to the panel members. Each group of the four groups will be responsible for the appropriate goal using the following guidelines.

A OPENING (ORAL PRESENTATION)

The first four minutes will be the opening presentation during which the group will present orally the most significant information from its part of the portfolio.

1. It should be based on the portfolio display and documentation section, but should not be a word-for-word reading from the display.
2. Use graphics from the portfolio to help you explain or emphasize a point.
3. Only materials included in your portfolio may be used during the oral presentation. You may not introduce additional materials such as videotapes, slides, computer demonstrations, etc.

B FOLLOW-UP QUESTIONS

The next six minutes will be the follow-up question period during which a panel of evaluators will ask the group about its portfolio presentation. During this period the evaluators might ask you to

1. explain further or clarify points you have made
2. give examples of specific points you have made
3. defend some of your statements or positions
4. answer questions about what you learned from your experience. What problems did you have? What were the most important things you learned as you studied this community problem?

C PREPARATION

You might ask parents or other community members experienced in making public presentations to coach your group. People involved in local government or in civic and community organizations can be very helpful.

Practice your oral presentation prior to giving it to an adult audience. Try it out in front of your classmates or students from other classes.

D GUIDELINES

As many members of each group as possible should participate in the opening presentation and follow-up question period. The oral presentation should not be dominated by one or two students. It should demonstrate the cooperative learning that went into the portfolio preparation.

Do not read to the evaluators from your portfolio display. Select the most important information and arguments and present them in a conversational style.

You may use notes during the opening presentation but not during the follow-up question period.

If you do not use the full four minutes allowed for the opening presentation, the unused time will be added to the follow-up question period. Each group is entitled to ten minutes before the evaluators.

You may use only those materials included in your group's portfolio during your oral presentation.

E EVALUATION CRITERIA

If your class decides to enter your portfolio in a local Project Citizen Showcase in which there is an oral presentation, a panel of evaluators will rate your presentation. Your teacher will explain the criteria that will be used in rating the presentations.

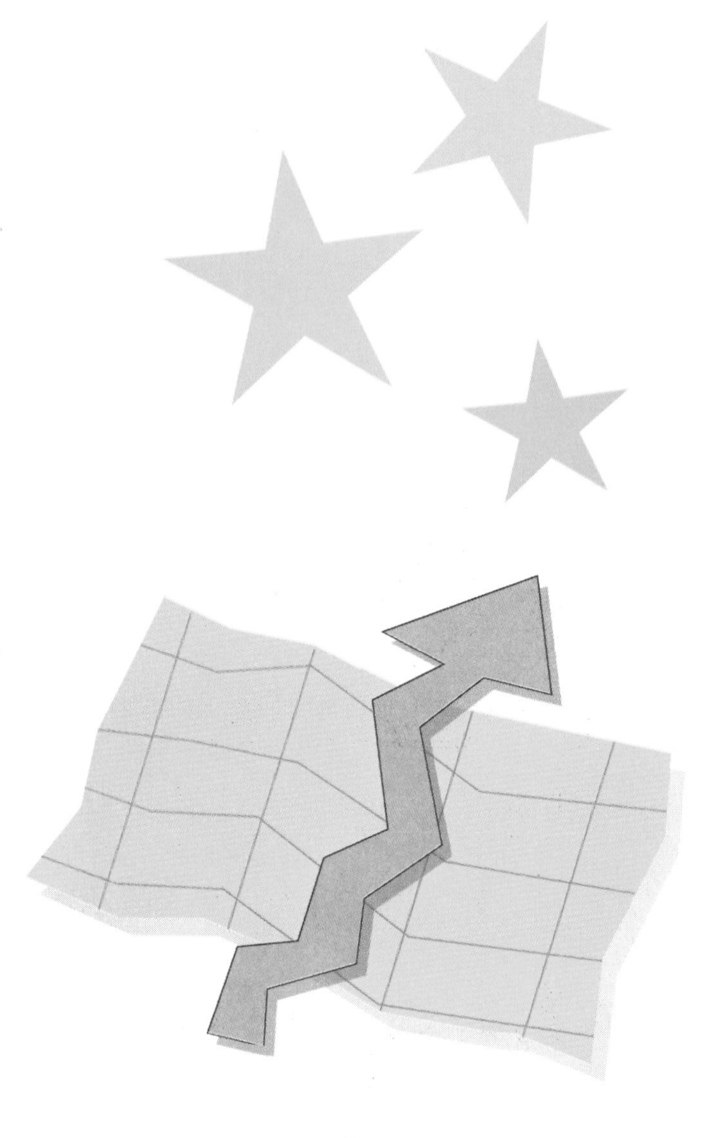

STEP 6

REFLECTING ON YOUR LEARNING EXPERIENCE

PURPOSE

It is always a good idea to think about or reflect on experiences you have had or projects you have completed. This is one way to learn, to avoid mistakes in the future, and to improve your performance.

REFLECTION

Now that your class has completed its portfolio, add a reflection or evaluation part to the Documentation Section binder. This part of your portfolio should describe briefly

- what and how you and your classmates learned
- what you might do differently if you were to develop another portfolio

Reflecting on your experiences should be a cooperative class effort similar to the way you have worked throughout this project. Reflect as an individual as well as a member of your class. Your teacher and the adults who helped you develop your portfolio can help you reflect on your experiences in this project.

It may be helpful to present your portfolio to an audience before your class develops this final part of your portfolio. Questions from members of an audience and their reactions to your portfolio may help you reflect on your learning experiences and the portfolio you developed.

CONCLUSION

It is important that you continue to develop the skills that help you influence the making of public policy. You will use these skills in the future. Remember that public policies often need to be revised. New problems require new public policies. Helping to develop public policies and taking positions on them are lifelong responsibilities of citizens in a self-governing society.

GUIDELINES - POSSIBLE QUESTIONS FOR REFLECTION

You may use the following questions to reflect on your experience.

1. What did I personally learn about public policy from working with my classmates?
2. What did we learn as a class about public policy by developing our portfolio?
3. What skills did I acquire or improve on in this project?
4. What skills did we acquire or improve on in this project?
5. What are the advantages of working as a team?
6. What are the disadvantages of working as a team?
7. What did I do well?
8. What did we do well?
9. How can I improve my problem-solving skills?
10. How can we improve our problem-solving skills?
11. What would we want to do differently if we were to develop another portfolio on another public policy issue?

GLOSSARY

The words in the glossary are defined to clarify their meaning as used in this text. Additional terms have been included because they relate to civics and are commonly used in the study of government and the making of public policy. Refer to your dictionary for more complete definitions.

abstract A summary of the most important points in a document such as a newspaper article.

administration Day-to-day management of public policies and procedures.

administrative agencies Departments of a government that manage the daily affairs of that government or other institutions.

alternative policies Any number of possible courses of action for dealing with a particular need or problem.

analysis The process of examining a subject in detail by studying its parts.

basic liberties Freedoms that are fundamental to democratic societies, such as freedom of religion, freedom of expression, and due process of law.

bill A proposed law submitted to a legislature.

citizen A member of a nation who is entitled to the rights and privileges of membership and who has the duties and responsibilities of membership (citizenship).

city government The political unit of authority responsible for making, carrying out, and enforcing city laws.

city inspectors Employees of city government who check to ensure that laws and regulations are being followed.

civic Of a citizen or citizens.

community organizations Groups of community members working toward common goals.

community standards Levels of acceptable behavior agreed to by individuals living in a city or community.

congressional district One of the 435 defined areas of the United States, each with approximately 500,000 people, that elects one congressperson to the U.S. House of Representatives.

constitutionality The state of being permitted according to the U.S. Constitution.

coordination Working together efficiently.

criteria The rules or qualifications that are used for judging.

demonstrate To show how something is done.

display section The part of the portfolio that is mounted for an audience to view. It provides an overview of the entire portfolio.

documentation section The part of the portfolio that contains selected records of the team's research as well as their original papers.

enforce To make people obey laws and public policies.

ethnic group A cultural group often defined by shared ancestry, heritage, and customs.

excerpt A passage or section taken out of a book or other publication.

exhibit A document or other object formally submitted as evidence to support a position.

gender Classification of people as either male or female.

governmental agency A part or division of the executive branch of local, state, or national government responsible for carrying out and enforcing laws and other public policies.

graphic presentations Pictures or diagrams that give a clear visual impression of the main points of the portfolio.

interest group A group of persons having a common interest or goal.

interview A conversation for the purpose of obtaining facts and other information.

issue A subject being discussed or disputed.

laws Rules that are created and enforced by governments.

legislative offices Lawmakers and their staffs.

legislature A group of persons chosen by the voters to make laws.

lobbyists People who present the interests of particular groups to lawmakers in order to influence them.

local government Political units of authority serving the needs of a city, town, borough, county, etc.

oral Spoken rather than written.

persuasiveness The power to convince others.

policy A plan of action designed to achieve a certain goal.

practicality The state of being realistic rather than idealistic.

professor A teacher at a college or university.

public policy An agreed-upon way that our government fulfills its responsibilities, such as its responsibilities to protect the rights of individuals and promote the welfare of all the people. Some public policies are written into laws by legislatures. Other policies are contained in rules and regulations created by administrative branches of government—the branches responsible for carrying out and enforcing laws.

reflection Serious thought or meditation.

scholar Someone who has done advanced study or research in a particular field.

source A document or a person that supplies information.

specifications A list giving exact descriptions.

statistics Numerical data.

United States Congress The legislature of the United States, consisting of the Senate and House of Representatives.

values Something that people think is of great importance such as freedom, justice, or loyalty. Values provide standards used in judging behavior. For example, honesty is a value used to judge a person's behavior.

zoning Local rules that divide a community into areas and tell how the land in each area can be used.

zoning department An agency of local government that determines and regulates the use of land for a particular purpose such as for homes, businesses, or recreation.

APPENDIX A LIBRARIES

The following are examples of libraries in the Los Angeles area. Use a telephone directory to find libraries in your community or ask an adult to help you find your local library using the Internet.

Commerce Public Library
323.722.6660
5655 Jillson Street
Commerce, CA 90040

Los Angeles Public Library
213.228.7000
630 W. Fifth Street
Los Angeles, CA 90071

Pasadena Public Library
626.744.4066
285 E. Walnut Street
Pasadena, CA 91101

University of Southern California Crocker Business Library
213.740.8520
201 Hoffman Hall
701 Exposition Boulevard
University of Southern California
Los Angeles, CA 90089

West Los Angeles Regional Branch Library
310.575.8323
11360 Santa Monica Boulevard
Los Angeles, CA 90025

APPENDIX B NEWSPAPERS

The following are examples of newspapers and their websites that you can use to find information on the problem you are studying. Ask a librarian or another adult to help you find and use these newspapers' websites. You may find that your local newspaper is the best source for news about local problems.

Atlanta Journal–Constitution
404.526.5151
72 Marietta Street
Atlanta, GA 30303
www.ajc.com

Chicago Tribune
312.222.3232
435 N. Michigan Avenue
Chicago, IL 60611
www.chicagotribune.com

Christian Science Monitor
617.450.2000
One Norway Street
Boston, MA 02115
www.csmonitor.com

Cleveland Plain Dealer
216.999.4800
1801 Superior Avenue
Cleveland, OH 44114
www.cleveland.com/plaindealer

New York Times
212.556.1234
229 W. 43rd Street
New York, NY 10036
www.nytimes.com

APPENDIX C COMMUNITY/ INTEREST GROUPS

The following are examples of community and interest groups. You can find other community and interest groups in a local telephone directory or by asking a librarian or another adult to help you find them on the Internet.

Orange Chamber of Commerce and Visitor Bureau
714.538.3581
439 E. Chapman Avenue
Orange, CA 92866

San Bernardino Area Chamber of Commerce
909.885.7515
546 W. Sixth Street
San Bernardino, CA 92402

San Diego Regional Chamber of Commerce
619.544.1300
402 W. Broadway, Suite 1000
San Diego, CA 92101

Latin Business Association
213.628.8510
120 S. San Pedro Street, Suite 530
Los Angeles, CA 90012

Vietnamese Chamber of Commerce
714.892.6928
9121 Bolsa Avenue, Suite 203
Westminster, CA 92683

League of Women Voters of Los Angeles
213.368.1616
3250 Wilshire Boulevard, Suite 1005
Los Angeles, CA 90010

National Center for American Indian Enterprise Development
626.442.3701
11138 Valley Mall, Suite 200
El Monte, CA 91731

Sierra Club–Angeles Chapter
213.387.4287
3435 Wilshire Boulevard, Suite 320
Los Angeles, CA 90010